For My Special Friend, MT

Memories of our friendship!

Sue

# LAMBERTVILLE

YVONNE WARREN & LOU TOBOZ
PHOTOGRAPHY
WALTER CHOROSZEWSKI

PUBLISHED BY
YVONNE WARREN & LOU TOBOZ

IN ASSOCIATION WITH
AESTHETIC PRESS, INC.
SOMERVILLE, NEW JERSEY

*Dedicated to the people of Lambertville.*

## YVONNE WARREN

Yvonne Warren, a resident of Lambertville for 17 years, has a zeal for recording the history of the city via books, photos and videos. She serves as Consulting Historian to the Lambertville Historical Society and has taken an active role in the operation of the James Marshall House Museum.

## LOU TOBOZ

Lou Toboz, a New Jersey native, has lived in Lambertville since 1978. He has an ongoing interest in the city and its people. He is an active participant in many civic groups and organizations. Lou is presently the City Historian and past president of the Lambertville Historical Society.

## WALTER CHOROSZEWSKI

Award-winning photographer, Walter Choroszewski, has been capturing the best of New Jersey since 1980, and has published numerous books and calendars on the state. Walter, his wife, Susan, and son, Joe, are frequent visitors to their favorite river town of Lambertville.

## LAMBERTVILLE

## ISBN 0-933605-07-2

## AESTHETIC PRESS, INC.,

Box 5306, Somerville, NJ 08876-1303 TEL: 908 369-3777

Net-hauling shad on
the Delaware River.

*T*he land occupied by Lambertville was originally purchased from the Delaware Indians as a portion of the 150,000 acre tract along the Delaware River. The flat nearest the river was an Indian camp location. The settlement of the town began with John Holcombe who purchased 350 acres in 1705 and made it his place of residence.

The second settler was Emanuel Coryell who arrived 27 years later and bought land next to Holcombe's. It included the ferry site by which those traveling York Road from Philadelphia could cross the Delaware River and continue across New Jersey to New York City. Coryell opened a tavern and inn to provide service to travelers using the Swift Sure Stage Line.

The settlement was called Coryell's Ferry for 80 years. During the Revolution, Coryell's Ferry served as an outpost and crossing point three times for General Washington and his troops. The property of these first two settlers was inherited by the sons who remained in Coryell's Ferry throughout their lifetimes.

By 1746, the Lambert family settled to the north of Holcombe's land. In 1812, John Lambert built a stone tavern and inn on Bridge Street that today is the restored Lambertville House. John Lambert's uncle became a member of the United States Senate during Thomas Jefferson's presidency. The Senator procured the first post office and proceeded to change the name of Coryell's Ferry to Lambert's Ville after his own family. Later the name evolved to Lambertville.

In 1830, the Delaware and Raritan Canal was chartered to connect the Delaware and Raritan Rivers. A 22-mile feeder canal was built from Trenton through Lambertville to tap water from the river at Raven Rock.

The 1863 map of the area shows 516 structures with a population of 2,851 people. During the Civil War many Lambertville men became volunteers, and a monument located in Mary E. Sheridan Park commemorates their efforts.

In the 1870s and 1880s, Lambertville contained a variety of businesses, ranging from single-person operations to factories that manufactured products 24 hours per day. Train service which began in 1851 connected these factories with major rail lines in Trenton, transporting Lambertville's products to domestic markets and also to the ports of New York and Philadelphia, reaching international markets.

At the beginning of this century, Lambertville's flourishing industries ranged from rubber to hair pins; from silk to locomotives. When factories closed, other companies soon moved in and adapted the buildings to their use. The economic changes from the 1920s through the WWII years forced many of these factories into decades of dormancy, only to be awakened in the 1980s and 1990s. Saved from demolition, many of these early buildings were restored and now are home to viable new businesses.

Many Federal and Victorian-era houses of the city were also spared from destruction. As the end of the 20th century draws near, Lambertville is resplendent with restored beautiful homes on its tree-lined streets.

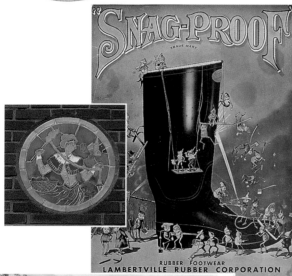

RUBBER FOOTWEAR
LAMBERTVILLE RUBBER CORPORATION CO.

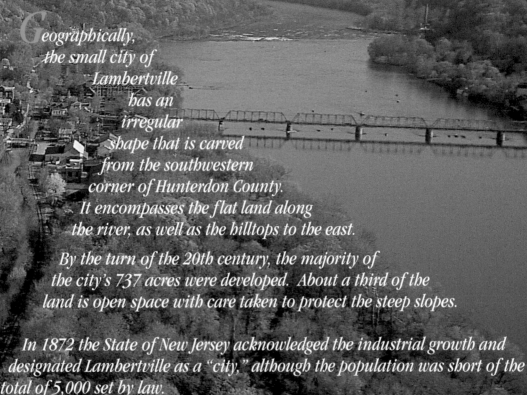

*G*eographically,
the small city of
Lambertville
has an
irregular
shape that is carved
from the southwestern
corner of Hunterdon County.
It encompasses the flat land along
the river, as well as the hilltops to the east.

By the turn of the 20th century, the majority of
the city's 737 acres were developed. About a third of the
land is open space with care taken to protect the steep slopes.

In 1872 the State of New Jersey acknowledged the industrial growth and
designated Lambertville as a "city," although the population was short of the
total of 5,000 set by law.

Lambertville is located fifteen miles north of Trenton, the state capital. William
Trent had settled the river town that took and kept his name some years before
Emanuel Coryell established his ferry crossing up river from "Trent's Town". Over the
centuries, Trenton's ties with Lambertville were many. Lambertville residents found
employment in Trenton, while proximity to Trenton aided the businesses of Lambertville
as the city developed into an industrial complex and transportation center.

The Lewis Family has been net-hauling shad
on the Delaware River for over 100 years.
Scenes of Fred Lewis [blue shirt] and his
crew in the late 1980s.

Celebrating the annual return of the migrating shad, the first festival in 1981 began as a small art show. Today, Shad Fest is a nationally recognized event that attracts thousands to Lambertville each spring, for arts & crafts, food and fun.

Left - Dining under a "starry night"
at Manon, N. Union St.
Right - 4th of July Celebration.
Right Inset - Dining at
Lambertville Station, Bridge St.

Left - Backyard play, N. Union St.
Left Inset - Family time at Ely Field.
Right - Swinging at Cavallo Park.

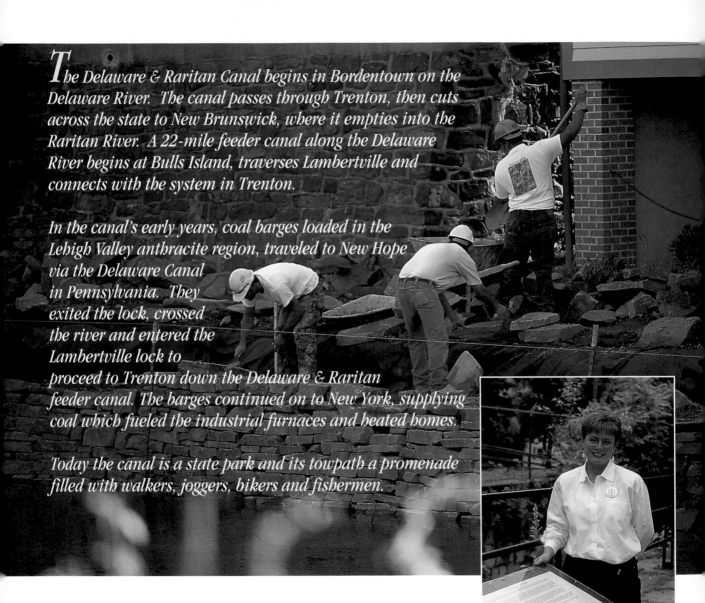

*The Delaware & Raritan Canal begins in Bordentown on the Delaware River. The canal passes through Trenton, then cuts across the state to New Brunswick, where it empties into the Raritan River. A 22-mile feeder canal along the Delaware River begins at Bulls Island, traverses Lambertville and connects with the system in Trenton.*

*In the canal's early years, coal barges loaded in the Lehigh Valley anthracite region, traveled to New Hope via the Delaware Canal in Pennsylvania. They exited the lock, crossed the river and entered the Lambertville lock to proceed to Trenton down the Delaware & Raritan feeder canal. The barges continued on to New York, supplying coal which fueled the industrial furnaces and heated homes.*

*Today the canal is a state park and its towpath a promenade filled with walkers, joggers, bikers and fishermen.*

Above - Restoration of canal wall.
Right - Robin Boyle, canal advocate.
Far Right - Sunday afternoon
on the D&R Canal.

16

Above - York Street
Bed & Breakfast, York St.
Right - The Apple Inn, York St.

Above - 44 Coryell
Bed & Breakfast, Coryell St.

Left - River Ballet
Academy, S. Main St.
Above- Town geese.
Right - Autumn reflections
on the D&R Canal.

Left - Artist, Bernard Ungerleider.
Below- Artist, Suzanne Douglass.
Right - Artist, Betsy Love.

Familiar Faces.
Left Top - Don Lewis, well-known resident.
Above - Miss Allonia, community leader.
Left  - Mary & John Williams,
The Merchantile, N. Main St.

Familiar Faces.
Right - Andrew Closson,
Homestead Farm Market.
Far Right - Julio Lopez, Postman.
Below - Ed Carmody,
community volunteer.

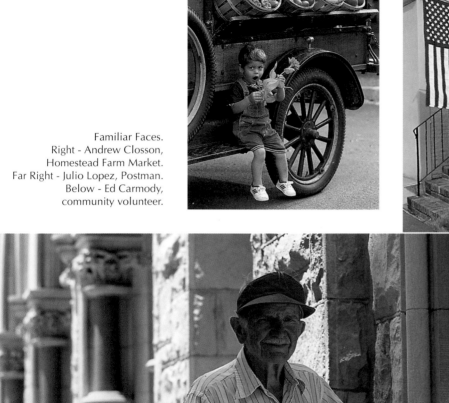

Lambertville's wing dam
provides high water delight
for kayakers, and during low
water it is a gathering place
for many river pleasures.

Left - Walking bike across the "Free Bridge."
Above - Bikers on the canal towpath.
Following - Dawn's reflections in the Delaware River.

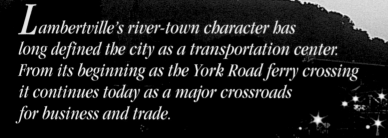

*Lambertville's river-town character has long defined the city as a transportation center. From its beginning as the York Road ferry crossing it continues today as a major crossroads for business and trade.*

*From the "Free Bridge," pedestrians can take in the river views and have an ideal vantage point for watching Lambertville's swallows, geese, ducks, jet skiers, boat racers, tubers, scullers and fishermen that share the river.*

N. Union St. architecture.
Left- Tuscan Revival Mansion.
Right - Lambertville Vernacular
which was the model for the
"Discover NJ History"
license plate [above].

Left-  Painting, Bridge St.
Right - Painting, Coryell St.

Top - Swan Creek
Rowing Club.
Right - Scenes from the
Swan Creek Rowing Club
Invitational Regatta.

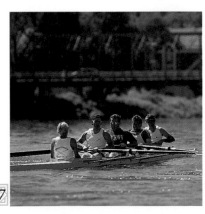

Left - Tuscan
Revival Mansion,
Jefferson St.
& George St.
Right - Italian
Revival Mansion,
S. Union St.
& Mt. Hope St.

38

 Left - Historic Marshall
House,Bridge St.
Top - Bedroom.
Right - Parlor.
Folllowing - Autumn
colors on Lewis Island.

41

Above - Porch Flags,
N. Union St.
Right - Antique
shop, Lambert Lane.
Far Right - Civil War
Monument, Mary E.
Sheridan Park, York St.

The Black River &
Western Railroad
runs between
Flemington and
Lambertville.

*N*ew industries sprang up in Lambertville when it was announced that a railroad would be built to parallel the river and the canal. Train service began in 1851 and was extended up river to join the northern rail network system. For over a century the railroad served Lambertville's industrial complex. Today an occasional steam train brings weekend tourists to enjoy destination Lambertville.

Above - Lamppost
ornament, N. Union St.
Right - Horse & Carriage
near Lambertville Station.

48

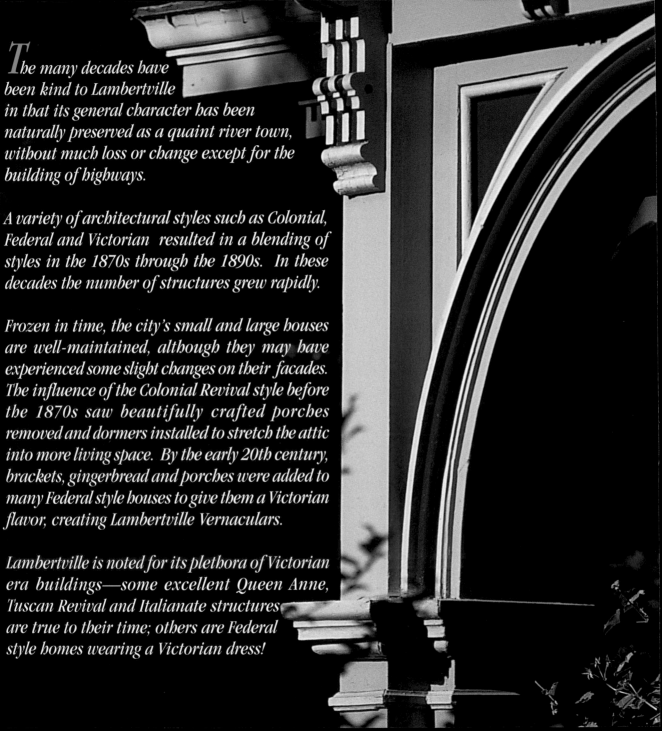

*The many decades have been kind to Lambertville in that its general character has been naturally preserved as a quaint river town, without much loss or change except for the building of highways.*

*A variety of architectural styles such as Colonial, Federal and Victorian resulted in a blending of styles in the 1870s through the 1890s. In these decades the number of structures grew rapidly.*

*Frozen in time, the city's small and large houses are well-maintained, although they may have experienced some slight changes on their facades. The influence of the Colonial Revival style before the 1870s saw beautifully crafted porches removed and dormers installed to stretch the attic into more living space. By the early 20th century, brackets, gingerbread and porches were added to many Federal style houses to give them a Victorian flavor, creating Lambertville Vernaculars.*

*Lambertville is noted for its plethora of Victorian era buildings—some excellent Queen Anne, Tuscan Revival and Italianate structures are true to their time; others are Federal style homes wearing a Victorian dress!*

Above - Milk bottle display,
Holcombe-Jimison Farm Museum.
Left -   Kegs at the
River Horse Brewery, Lambert Lane.
Right - Bar scene,
The Inn of the Hawke, Mt. Hope St.

Dottie, Coryell St.

Perry, Perry St.

Harry, George St.

Jazz, George St.

Pets of Lambertville. 54

Maggie, N. Union St.

Joey, Coryell St.

Patches, Coryell St.

Jake, N. Union St.

Left - Niece Lumber, Elm St.
Below - Antiques display, N. Union St.

Above - Holcombe-Jimison
Farm Museum, Daniel Bray Highway.

Left - Scenes along the D&R Canal.
Top - Coffee break, Lambertville.
Trading Company, Bridge St.
Above - Curbside Sno-Cones, Bridge St.
Right - City Hall, York St.

Left - Kalmia Club, York St.
Above - Garden detail, York St.
Right - Porches, Delaware Ave.

Top - Youth League
baseball at Ely Field.
Left - Scenes from Youth
League, and men's and
women's softball at Ely Field.

Left - Opening reception
at the Artists' Gallery, Coryell St.
Above - Coryell Gallery, Coryell St.

Wood and metal fences
bordering the homes and
businesses of Lambertville.

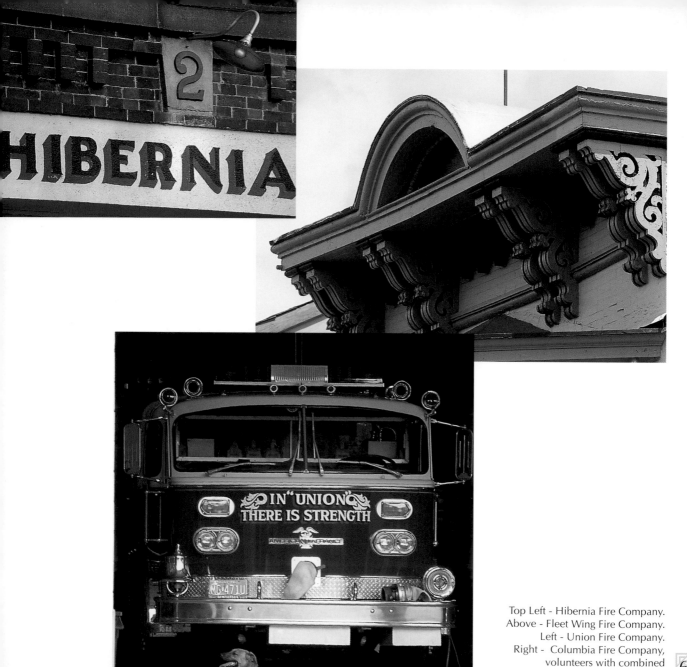

Top Left - Hibernia Fire Company.
Above - Fleet Wing Fire Company.
Left - Union Fire Company.
Right - Columbia Fire Company,
volunteers with combined
service of 248 years.

Lambertville has numerous
private showcase gardens.

ATTENTION
CHIEN BIZARRE

THE
BOAT HOUSE

The Porkyard

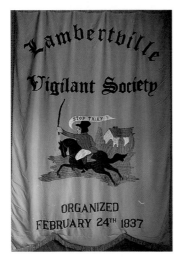

Lambertville
Vigilant Society

STOP THIEF

ORGANIZED
FEBRUARY 24TH 1837

FINKLES

FIRST BAPTIST CHURCH
1869

W

Left - Lambertville
Station, Bridge St.
Right - Shops along Bridge St.

74

Above - Morning on the porch at
The Lambertville House, Bridge St.
Right - Breakfast display,
The Bridge Street House, Bridge St.
Following - Walking across the "Free Bridge."

*L*ambertville's central business district offers a mix of storefronts and homes, interesting shop signs, attractive window displays, and people crowding the sidewalks. The hum of the city emanates from the busy individuals keeping the menagerie of shops and plenty of food ready for the home folk and visitors.

In such a small city, it is difficult, if not impossible, to be anonymous within the community. The population is about 4,000 living in some 1,700 homes within a 1.1 square mile. There is no escape from contact with neighbors in this intimate, old-fashioned American city.

To find easy avenues into the sense of community, there are many opportunities, such as involvement with churches, lodges, organizations and athletic teams. Porches, back yards and not-so-secret gardens set scenes for over-the-fence visiting. Community-wide picnics, block parties and parades are held often, and are all great crowd pleasers.

"Born in Lambertville" residents have an advantage of knowing whose relative is whose. Even some out-of-towners become known too—especially if they shop regularly in stores like Finkle's Hardware, Niece Lumber and Ben Franklin; or stop at Sneddons or the Lambertville Trading Company for lunch or coffee.

There appears to be a great interest in watching others work. One sidewalk ritual is to watch the progress of a restoration job. Perhaps a contractor needs help in finding a spot he missed! Workers often end up with other helpful hints and recommendations from the sidewalk experts.

The reuse of classic buildings for art galleries, antique shops, restaurants and unique businesses adds to the "old charm" of today's Lambertville.

# SPONSORS

David Rago Auction, Inc., David Rago
Hamilton's Grill Room, Jim Hamilton
Pinch Penny and Dress Well, Marty Luther & Marcia Chapman

5 & DIME, Steve Stegman & Paul Corpering
A MANO Galleries, Martin & Ana Leyland
The Apple Inn, Bed & Breakfast, Ginny Lee
Archangel Antiques, Joe Cavallaro
Art Craft, Fred Schmitz
Automatic Musical Instruments, C. Alan Lightcap
Bear Apothecary Shoppe, Mort Barnett
Peg Beech, Realtor, ERA - Burgdorff Realtors
Bell's Union Street Restaurant & Bar
Ben Franklin, Joe & Edith Musselman
Betsy Love, Painter & Tilemaker
Allan Blauth, Architect
Blue Raccoon Home & Garden, Nicholas Bewsey & Nelson Zayas
The Boat House, Inc., Jim Bulger
Buchanan Construction
Gustavo Calderon, M.D.
Carman's Collectables, Carolyn R. Asness
Contractor's Supply Company, Tom Briggs
Jim Cook & Jim Richardson
Coryell Gallery, Janet Marsh Hunt
Bonnie Eick, Realtor, E. J. Lelie Agency
Fran Jay's Glass, Fran & Marvin Silverstein
Steven Frankel
Full Moon Restaurant, Jacqueline Bowe
Jean Galloway, Broker, John T. Henderson, Inc.
Garden House Antiques, Delyn McCosh, Laurie Humm, Deloris Verchere

Garefino Funeral Home, Charles Garefino
Lisa Gladden and Brian, Ross & John Keys
The Golden Rhino
Goldsmiths, Roger Thompson
Gordon Haas Gallery & Studio
June E. Grutzmacher, M.D., F.A.C.S.
H & C Antiques, Henry & Carolyn Eick
Vivian Hackney, Realtor, E. J. Lelie Agency
Pat & Bruce Hamilton
Hart Enterprises, Don Hart
Heath's Exxon Service, Bob Heath
Helena Castella Antiques & Fine Furnishings
Homestead Farm Market, Ed & Debbie Closson
Ginny Hook, Realtor, E. J. Lelie Agency
Hrefna Jonsdottir Gallery
The Inn of the Hawke, Doreen & Melissa Masset
J. B. Kline & Son, George R. Kline
Joanna Hearts - *Romantic Home Accessories & Gifts*
Joseph Finkle & Son, Inc. - *Service since 1912*
Keen, Yanarella & Trautz Partners
Kelly McDowell's Estate Jewelry & Antiques
The Lambertville House - *A National Historic Inn*
Lambertville Optical, Ray Marfino
Lambertville Pharmacy
The Lambertville Station
Lambertville Trading Company, Lisa & Dean Stephens
Lewis Fishery, Steve Meserve
Catherine Lundie & Todd Stine
Tom McMillan, Realtor, R. A. Weidel Corp.
Meld, Jose A. Chacon
The Merchantile, John & Mary Williams
Mildred's Salon, Mildred Rock

Steven H. Morland, Jr., Attorney
News Travels, Paul A. Gingold, CTC
Niece Lumber - *Since 1920*
One Stitch at a Time, Cathie Giambalvo
Suzanne & Ed Padilla
Stewart Palilonis, Attorney at Law
Peter Wallace, Ltd, Dan Margo
Protocol Electronics, Inc., Jay B. Ross
Reinboth & Company
Richard A. Weidel Corporation, Realtors
Rick's Restaurant, Rick & Katrin Buscavage
River Ballet Academy
River Horse Brewing Company, Jack, Jim & Tim Bryan
Rivergate Books, Janet Holbrook
Riverrun Gallery, Grace Croteau
Ronald R. Tillett & Sons, Inc.
Salon Bruno, Robin Boyle & Fred Riga
Tish Secula, Realtor, R. A. Weidel Corp.
Jim & Barbara Siuta
Mary Rittenhouse Smith
Sojourner, Amy Coss
Sports & Optimal Performance Psychology, Dr. James. L. Mastrich, Jr.
Standin' Room Only, Steve Williamson
Stefon's Antiques, Bob Due
The Swan Hotel, Inc., Jim Bulger
Sylvester's
Bernard Ungerleider Studio
The Urban Archeologist, Seva Hiras & Mary Louise Venettone
Van Horn - McDonough Funeral Home, Richard McDonough
Michelle & Dan Walsky
Welsh's Wines, Dick Welsh
York Street House Bed & Breakfast, Nancy Ferguson & Beth Wetterskog

Lambertville's church steeples
viewed from Mt. Hope Cemetery.